CONTENTS

Peace At Last
by Jill Murphy

CREDITS

Published by Scholastic Ltd,
Villiers House,
Clarendon Avenue,
Leamington Spa,
Warwickshire CV32 5PR
Text © Hilary Braund and Deborah Campbell
© 1999 Scholastic Ltd
  2 3 4 5 6 7 8 9 0   9 0 1 2 3 4 5 6 7 8

Authors Hilary Braund and Deborah Campbell
Editor Kate Pearce
Series designer Lynne Joesbury
Designer Rachael Hammond
Illustrations Jill Murphy and Lynda Murray
Cover illustration Jill Murphy

Designed using Adobe Pagemaker

British Library Cataloguing-in-Publication Data
A catalogue record for this book is available from
the British Library.

ISBN 0-590-53983-3

ACKNOWLEDGEMENTS

Macmillan Children's Books Ltd, London for the
use of text and illustrations from Peace at Last by
Jill Murphy © Text and illustrations, 1980,
Jill Murphy (1980, Macmillan Children's Books).

INTRODUCTION

Peace At Last
by Jill Murphy

What's the plot of the story?
The Bear family are all ready for bed but Mr. Bear cannot sleep and is kept awake by Mrs. Bear's snoring. He gets up to find somewhere quiet to sleep. But is there anywhere that isn't noisy?

What's so good about this book?
Peace At Last is an excellent book for reading aloud and has plenty of opportunities for children to participate. The repetition allows children to tackle the book independently and the text is strongly supported by the illustrations. The full colour pictures support the text while the black and white line drawings add detail beyond the written story.

About Jill Murphy
Jill Murphy was born in London and since the age of three has been writing and illustrating books. She wrote and illustrated one of her best-known stories *The Worst Witch* at the age of eighteen, although this was not actually published until several years later.

For two years Jill Murphy worked in a children's home and *Peace at Last* grew from a story she told a small boy as she was taking him to playgroup. *Peace at Last* remains her favourite and earned her a commendation in the Kate Greenaway awards.

Introducing the book

Learning intentions

● to build awareness of authorship
● to make predictions about story content using information from the front cover
● to relate story themes to events in the children's own lives

Organization

● whole class

Look at the front cover with the children. Read the title to them and tell them that the author is Jill Murphy. Ask if they know any other stories by this person.

Read aloud the first two paragraphs from the blurb on the back cover. Ask the children:

● *What other noises might keep Mr. Bear awake?*
● *Have you heard the expression 'Peace at last' before? What does it mean?*
● *How might the expression 'Peace at last' relate to this story?*

● *How does Mr. Bear look on the front cover? Do you think this might give you a clue as to how the story ends?*

Look at the picture in the book showing the Bear family on the sofa and ask:

● *What time is shown on the clock?*
● *What time do you go to bed?*
● *What do you and your family do before going to bed?*
● *What other stories about bears do you know? Can you find any more in the classroom?*

Reading the story

Learning intentions
● to predict story incidents
● to recognize repeated phrases within the story
● to link story themes to their own experiences

Organization
● whole class

Explain to the class that you are going to read the story to them but that you will be stopping to ask questions as you read.

Read up to 'Mrs. Bear fell asleep. Mr. Bear didn't'. Ask the children: *Do you know any good ways of getting to sleep?* Carry on reading up to where Baby Bear is pretending to be an aeroplane. *What do you do when you go to bed? Do you go straight to sleep?*

Read up to '...went the refrigerator'. *What do you think Mr. Bear might say? Where do you think he went after that?*

Read up to '...what noises there are in the garden at night'.

Look at the illustration with the class. *What noises do you think kept Mr. Bear awake?*

Look at the picture of Mr. Bear in the car then read up to '...was so tired that he didn't notice'. *What has happened to the sky? What time of day is it?*

Carry on reading up to '"Peace at last," he said to himself.' Ask the children: *Do you think that is the end of the story?*

Read to the end of the book. *Did you enjoy the story. What was your favourite part? Have you ever had trouble getting to sleep like Mr. Bear? What do you do if you can't get to sleep?*

What happens next?

Learning intentions
● to retell or invent stories giving the main points in a sequence
● to compare oral versions with the written text

Organization
● small group
● individual copies of photocopiable page 7 plus an enlarged copy for demonstration with the class

Cut the enlarged copy of photocopiable page 7 into six individual pictures. Invite the children to help you to make up an alternative version of the story by placing the pictures in any order they choose. When this is completed ask: *Does the sequence of events still make sense? Would the sequence make sense if you started the story with the alarm clock going off?*

Give each child a copy of photocopiable page 7 and a strip of paper and ask them to cut out the pictures and then glue them onto the paper in their chosen order. They can either retell the story in the same order as in the book or create their own version using the same events. The finished series of pictures can be used for oral storytelling or the children may like to write their own version of the story to accompany the illustrations.

True or false?

Learning intentions
● to recall information given in the text and implied in the illustrations

Organization
● individual or pairs
● copies of photocopiable pages 8 and 9

Give each child a copy of photocopiable pages 8 and 9 and read through the statements with the children. Explain that

some of the statements are true and some are not. Ask the children to work individually or in pairs. Explain that they should cut out each of the statements and then, using the grid on photocopiable page 9, stick them underneath the correct heading. The children can refer to the book to check the accuracy of their work. When they have done this, invite them to make up some true and false statements of their own to write under each heading.

What happens next?

Mrs Bear went to sleep.

The alarm clock woke Mr. Bear up.

Baby Bear went straight to sleep.

"Woof, woof," went the dog.

The car was very warm.

Mr. Bear couldn't sleep.

Mr. Bear went into the dining room.

Mr. Bear went to sleep in the car.

True or false? (2)

True	False

Do you know...?

Learning intentions
● to recall events in the story through asking and answering questions
● to use 'wh' words commonly used to open questions (such as what, where, when) and to use question marks appropriately

Organization
● small group
● copies of photocopiable page 11

Working with a small group of children, ask them these two questions about the story: *Where did Mr. Bear go when Mrs. Bear started to snore? What animals kept Mr. Bear awake in the garden?* When the children have answered these questions, invite them to think of others that they can ask the rest of the group.

Give each child a copy of photocopiable page 11 and explain how to cut them out to make lift-the-flap question and answer sheets (see the diagram below).

Look at question 1, which is already written on the sheet, and discuss the use of the question mark. Using a spare photocopiable sheet as an example, write the answer to the first question under the first flap. Tell the children that you want them to create their own questions on the remaining three flaps, writing their answers underneath each one.

The finished question and answer sheets can be shared with friends within the group or with the whole class.

Question 1: Where did Mr. Bear go when Mrs. Bear started to snore?   Question 2:

'Peace At Last'

Learning intentions
● to use awareness of sentence construction and the meaning of the story to predict missing words
● to use word recognition and phonic cues to select from a range of words

Organization
● whole class
● enlarged copy of photocopiable page 12

Using your enlarged copy of photocopiable page 12, cut out the words at the bottom of the sheet and attach Blu-Tack to the back of them.

Display the enlarged text and the individual words in a prominent position and explain to the class that you are going to work together to fill in the gaps with the correct words.

Read through the text with the children and ask them to predict the missing words. Invite children to select the appropriate words from the ones on offer and then to stick them in the correct places on the enlarged text. Discuss the cueing systems used, including phonic and contextual cues, to both predict and locate the missing words.

---

fold

Question 1:	Question 2:
Where did Mr. Bear go when Mrs. Bear started to snore?	*cut*

---

fold

Question 3:	Question 4:
	cut

'Peace at last'

In the ⬚ , Baby Bear was fast

asleep, and Mrs. Bear had turned

⬚ and wasn't ⬚

any more.

Mr. Bear got ⬚ bed and

⬚ his eyes.

"Peace at ⬚ ," he said

to ⬚ .

closed		
over	house	snoring
himself	into	last

What's that noise?

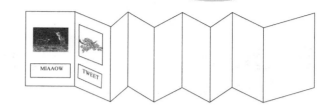

Learning intentions
● to discuss the story theme and make links with their own experiences
● to reinforce and apply word-level skills

Organization
● small group
● large sheet of paper
● copies of photocopiable page 14
● a nine page zig-zag book for each child

Ask the children to recall all the different sounds that kept Mr. Bear awake throughout the night. Write these on a large sheet of paper, asking the children to help with the spelling of the words, then read this list through with them. Ask them if they can think of other sounds that they hear that sometimes keep them awake at night. Suggestions might include *thunder, lorries driving past, car alarms, babies crying.*

Give each child a copy of photocopiable page 14 and a zig-zag book. Look at the pictures and read through the text together. Tell the children that you want them to cut out the text and illustrations. They should then match the text to the correct pictures and stick them into the zig-zag book. When they have done this, they should read their finished book back to a friend or to you.

The dawn chorus

Learning intentions
● to read for meaning in order to predict missing words
● to attempt own spelling of words
● to consider how alternative words can have similar meanings

Organization
● small group
● copies of photocopiable page 15

Give each child a copy of photocopiable page 15. Tell them to read the extract through and then to fill in the gaps using appropriate words. When they have finished, read through the children's completed work to ensure that it makes sense. Encourage them to compare their finished work with the text in the book. As a group share each child's work. Did everyone use the same words or were different words used in some places?

What's that noise?

NYAAOW! NYAAOW

MIAAOW!

TWEET TWEET

TICK-TOCK

HMMMMMM

BRRRRRRRRRR!

DRIP, DRIP

SNUFFLE, SNUFFLE

TOO-WHIT-TOO-WHOO

READ & RESPOND

14

The dawn chorus

It was _____ in the car and

uncomfortable, but Mr. Bear was so

_____ that he didn't notice.

He was just _____ asleep when all

_____ birds started to _____ and

the sun _____ in at the window.

"TWEET TWEET!" _____ the birds.

SHINE, SHINE ... went the _____ .

"Oh NO!" said Mr. _____ , "I can't

stand THIS."

So he got _____ and went back into

the _____ .

What's the time?

Learning intentions
● to build knowledge and understanding of story structure through considering the sequence of events and the passage of time
● to consider how illustrations add to the telling of the story

Organization
● whole class
● cut out blank clock-faces from photocopiable page 17

Look through the illustrations in the book with the children. Ask them to find all the clocks that are shown. *Can you tell what time is shown in each of them? What purpose do the clocks have in the telling of the story?*

Ensure the children understand the sequence of events as they are told in the book and the concept of chronology. On the pages where there are no clocks in the illustrations, ask the children to suggest times for clocks that could be shown on these pages. Draw the suggested times on the clock-faces available on photocopiable page 17. These can then be cut out and attached to the illustrations in the book with Blu-Tack.

What's the time, Mr. Bear?

Learning intentions
● to build understanding of the passage of time through events in the story
● to structure own writing based on a frame sentence

Organization
● small group
● copies of photocopiable page 18

Give each child a copy of photocopiable page 18 and look at the pictures and text it contains. Explain that you want them to add hands to the blank clock-faces to show the passage of time as Mr. Bear struggles through the night trying to get to sleep. (You may like to recap the work you have already done on sequencing and chronology.) They should also add a line of text to each of the pictures, using the frame sentence that is used in the first and last illustrations, 'At _____ o'clock...'.

What's the time?

MAKING SENSE

What's the time, Mr Bear?

At 9 o'clock the Bear family went to bed.

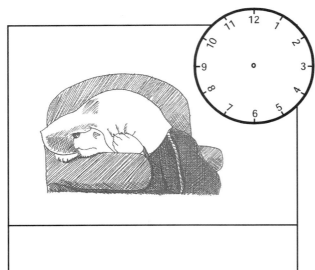

At 7 o'clock the alarm clock went off.

Story structure

Learning intentions
● to reflect on aspects of the story structure – characters, setting, events and themes

Organization
● whole class or small group
● copies of photocopiable page 20

Show the class or group a copy of photocopiable page 20 and explain that they are going to fill in the boxes. Talk about the headings in each box, explaining what they mean and, if necessary, sharing one example that could be included in each box.

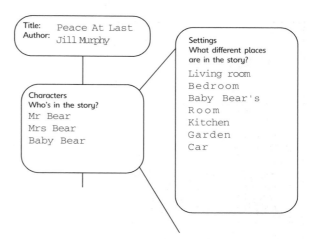

Hand out copies of the sheet and allow the children to work either individually or in pairs to complete it. The children could also add small illustrations to the written text in each box.

I can't stand THIS

Learning intentions
● to recognize and use aspects of print and punctuation in reading with expression

Organization
● whole class
● enlarged copy of photocopiable page 21

Show the children your enlarged copy of photocopiable page 21. Read it through in a monotone voice. Then ask the children if that is how it should be read or whether it could be read with greater feeling.

Ask them what they notice about the print on the page. Invite individual children to point out all the words written in capital letters. *What does this tell the reader about how they should be read aloud? Is there anything else that tells the reader what expression to use?* Draw the children's attention to the use of exclamation marks and ask them '…'. *Have you seen these forms of punctuation used before?*

Read the page through together again, this time using more appropriate expression.

Story structure

Title:
Author:

Settings
What different places
are in the story?

Characters
Who's in the story?

Events
What happens?

Favourite part of
the story

READ & RESPOND

TICK-TOCK ... went the living-room

clock ... TICK-TOCK, TICK-TOCK.

CUCKOO! CUCKOO!

"Oh NO!" said Mr. Bear,

"I can't stand THIS"

So he went off to sleep in the kitchen.

In the garden at night

Learning intentions
● to identify and use capital letters, full stops, exclamation marks and speech marks to bring meaning and expression to written text

Organization
● whole class
● large sheet of paper
● copies of photocopiable page 23

On a large sheet of paper write out the text on the page that begins 'DRIP, DRIP… ' but do not use any capital letters or punctuation. Invite children to come and add capital letters or punctuation where they feel it is appropriate. Recap on the correct terms for all the punctuation used. Compare the class's finished attempt with the text in the book. Have they forgotten anything or used alternatives?

Give each child a copy of photocopiable page 23. This is a copy of the text from the next page in the story, but without the capital letters or punctuation. Explain to the children that, working either alone or in pairs, you want them to add the missing details to the text. When they have finished, allow them to compare their own attempts with the text in the book.

In the garden at night

well you would not believe what

noises there are in the garden at night

too-whit-too-whoo went the owl

snuffle snuffle went the hedgehog

miaaow sang the cats on the wall

oh no said mr bear I can't stand this

so he went off to sleep in the car

Sound effects

Learning intentions
● to respond imaginatively to events in the story, using music or sound effects to add expression and atmosphere to their own retellings of the story

Organization
● whole class, followed by small groups
● collection of musical instruments
● tape recorder

Display the range of musical instruments that you have collected. Read through the story and invite children to suggest places where sound effects could be added. They can select from the range of instruments available or improvise sounds with other items from around the room.

A small group of children could then work together to create their own retelling of the story using sound effects. They may like to make a written record of the instruments that they use to accompany each section of the story, using either writing or symbols.

Make a tape recorder available so that the children can create their own story tapes along with sound effects for other children to use in the listening corner.

The Bears' house

Learning intentions
● to create storytelling props to support their own retelling of the story
● to explore the settings for the story

Organization
● pairs working within a small group
● sheets of A3 paper
● photocopiable page 25

Give each pair of children within a small group a sheet of A3 paper. Explain that you want them to choose one scene from the story to re-create and then to draw this on their paper. As a group, decide who is doing which scene to ensure there is no overlap. The children should draw or paint the background but not include the characters.

The finished pictures can be mounted on card and laminated. They can then be used for retelling the story using the characters cut out from photocopiable page 25.

The Bears' house

Mr. Bear

Mrs. Bear

Baby Bear

Where can Mr. Bear go?

Learning intentions
● to use similar story structures and form to create their own events

Organization
● whole class or small group
● Paper, drawing and writing materials

Recap the places in and around the house that Mr. Bear went in order to try to get some sleep. Ask the children if they can think of any other places that he could have tried, for example, the bathroom or the garage. Choose one of the suggestions and create some shared writing that includes that location in the story. For instance, *So he went off to sleep in the bathroom. The bath was very cold and slippery. RATTLE, RATTLE went the shaky bathroom window. "Oh NO," said Mr. Bear. "I can't stand THIS."*

Ask the children to draw a picture of their own alternative place where Mr. Bear could sleep and then to write up this addition to the story in their own words.

Every picture tells a story

Learning intentions
● to consider how the illustrations add detail and meaning to the story
● to use story-book language in oral storytelling

Organization
● whole class or small group
● multiple copies of the book (optional)

Prior to this activity decide whether you want to work with the whole class, inviting children to come out close to the book when contributing, or with a small group. (If you decide on group work this activity would work best if each child had a copy of the book.)

Explain to the children that they are going to be paying close attention to the illustrations in the book. Draw the children's attention both to the black and white illustrations and the full page colour illustrations. Discuss the relationship between the two types of pictures and the text.

Read the story through, pausing at the beginning of each section of text and invite the children to add detail to the story using the black and white illustrations. For example, *The Bear family had all had their cocoa. Mr. Bear was reading the paper, Mrs. Bear was knitting and Baby Bear was reading his favourite book.*

You could use the children's contributions in this activity as an opportunity to carry out some shared writing.

Peace at Last

Collect the sentence

Learning intentions
● to build familiarization with a repeated phrase from the story
● to create simple sentences

Organization
● small groups of no more than six children
● copies of photocopiable page 29
● photocopiable page 28 made up into a dice

Prior to the lesson, photocopy the net on page 28 onto card, cut it out and fold it into a dice.

Give each child a copy of photocopiable page 29 with the six words already cut into separate blocks. Ask the children what the bubble drawn on the page is for and if they can remember what Mr. Bear kept saying.

Explain that with the words you have cut out they have all the words to make the sentence 'Oh NO! I can't stand THIS.' They must take it in turns to roll the dice, collect the word that is shown and then place it in the right position in their speech bubble. Allow the children to play the game as a group.

When they have collected all the words, the children can glue them onto their own page in the right order to re-create the sentence. Alternatively, you could laminate the pictures and words so that they can be reused by subsequent groups.

Collect the sentence (1)

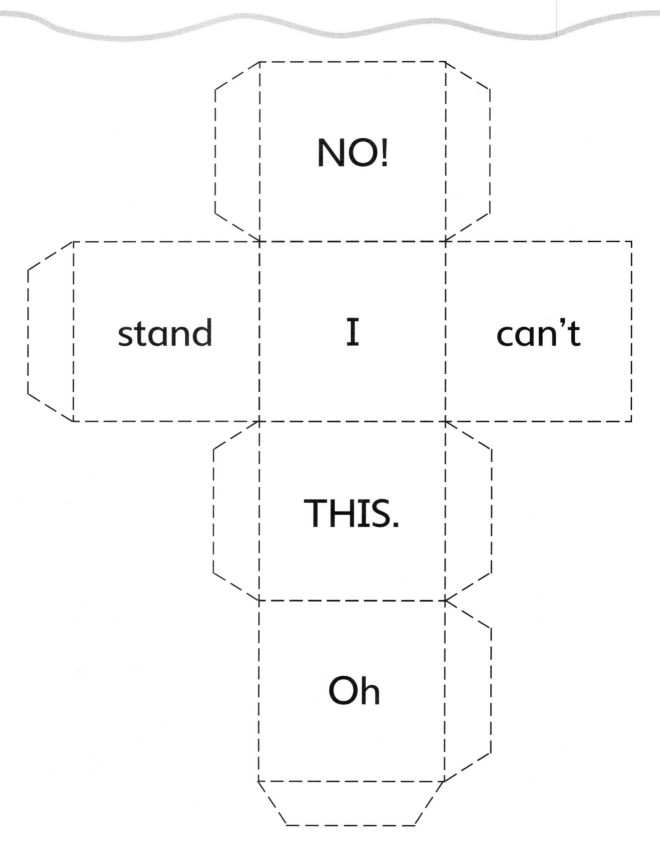

NO!

stand   I   can't

THIS.

Oh

| Oh | NO! | I | can't | stand | THIS. |

Helping Mr. Bear

Learning intentions
● to reflect on the events of the story
● to ask and answer questions about the events in the story

Organisation
● whole class

Either take on the role of Mr. Bear or, if the class are familiar with drama techniques, elect one of the children to take on this role. You can indicate when you are in role by sitting on a particular chair, or by leaving the carpet area and returning in role.

Mr. Bear announces to the class that he is very tired because he hardly got any sleep last night. Invite the children to ask him questions about why he couldn't sleep and also to offer suggestions as to how he might manage to get a good night's sleep in the future. For example, they may ask whether he has had any trouble sleeping before, what kind of noises kept him awake and what happened when he tried to sleep in the garden.

Their ideas for helping Mr Bear could be written up to make 'Mr. Bear's Book of How To Get To Sleep'.

Peace at Last

USING THIS BOOK

How to use this book

The activities in this book are designed to help develop the children's response to stories in the early stages of their literacy development. The emphasis is on text-level work; but many of the activities also provide opportunities for sentence- and word-level work.

The initial *Ways in* activity suggests ways of introducing the book to the children. Opportunities are provided for them to consider basic text conventions, such as the title, author and back cover blurb; and to develop strategies for making critical choices in selecting their own reading materials, by considering favourite authors and the use of the cover to provide clues as to the content of the story.

The *Making sense* activities focus on the immediate content of the book. The whole class activities allow you to explore with the children the ways in which meaning is communicated through the choice of vocabulary, the use of punctuation and aspects of the story structure. The group activities provide opportunities for children to explore these ideas in greater depth.

The *Developing ideas* activities allow the children to explore the story in different ways: through playing games, creative writing and art and music. The activities help the children to develop personal responses and encourage them to revisit the book on many occasions, feeling confident in their independent reading or retelling of the story.

The *Evaluation* activity uses the drama technique of 'hot-seating'. The children are encouraged to consider possible solutions to Mr. Bear's insomnia. This gives them an opportunity to practise their questioning skills in order to reflect on the theme of the story.

Classroom management

These activities can be used across a number of literacy sessions. It is suggested that the book be introduced through the *Ways in* activity, then read to the class as outlined on page 5. Further sessions could begin with a whole-class activity, followed by groups of children working on related activities, differentiated to individual needs.

Access to multiple copies of the book will enhance the children's learning opportunities in many of the activities, though several can also be successfully completed without direct access to the text. Those activities that require use of the book are indicated by the 📖 icon.

Including a range of activities within a single literacy session – whole class, small group with adult support and group or individual activities that can be completed independently – will make the session more manageable, and will help you to target particular learning intentions with chosen groups of children.

Differentiation

The activities are intended to cover the range of literacy development throughout Key Stage 1. Appropriate activities should be selected to meet the needs of groups of children. A number of the activities (both whole-class and group) can be differentiated by outcome and may therefore be suitable for children at all stages of literacy development.

Giving the children opportunities to report back on their work at the end of each session will allow them all to experience a wide range of activities, either directly or at second hand.

Linking activities

The *Making sense* activities include both whole class and group activities. In this book the four whole class activities are each followed by appropriate group activities which reinforce or extend similar learning intentions as shown in the following grid.

ACTIVITIES	GENERAL LEARNING INTENTIONS
READING THE STORY WHAT HAPPENS NEXT? TRUE OR FALSE DO YOU KNOW...?	• KNOWLEDGE OF THE STORY • RECALLING INFORMATION • ASKING AND ANSWERING QUESTIONS
PEACE AT LAST WHAT'S THAT NOISE? THE DAWN CHORUS	• WORD RECOGNITION • APPLYING APPROPRIATE CUEING SYSTEMS TO PREDICT UNKNOWN WORDS
WHAT'S THE TIME? WHAT'S THE TIME, MR. BEAR? STORY STRUCTURE	• FAMILIARISATION WITH STORY STRUCTURE - SEQUENCE, EVENTS, CHARACTERS, SETTINGS
I CAN'T STAND THIS IN THE GARDEN AT NIGHT	• USING FEATURES OF THE TEXT AND PUNCTUATION TO READ WITH EXPRESSION

Matching the book to your class

Peace At Last and its author Jill Murphy are established favourites in many primary classrooms. The story strongly supports early readers through the repetitive structure and strong visual cues. The theme is one to which the children may easily relate and provides ample opportunities for them to share their own experiences. It is an ideal book for reading aloud and revisiting on many occasions. As the children become more familiar with the story they enjoy joining in and taking over the reading.

Teaching potential of *Peace At Last*

The skills grid on the inside back cover outlines the areas of reading strategies, comprehension and response skills covered by the activities. Opportunities are also available for other learning intentions, many of which fulfil the teaching requirements of the National Literacy Strategy, while others provide cross-curricular links.

Recommended previous teaching

Children will need to be familiar with the idea of returning to a book several times to explore different aspects of it. They will also need to be used to working in groups on different activities – independently, collaboratively and with an adult.

Recommended classroom resources

For all activities it is assumed that the children will have access to writing and drawing materials. In addition many of the activities require access to general art materials and equipment, including glue, scissors, paints, and colouring pens and pencils. Specific resources for individual activities are listed under the **Organization** heading. *Peace At Last* is available in several bilingual versions.

Further reading
Books by Jill Murphy

Peace at Last (In English and Bengali, English and Chinese, English and Gujarati, English and Punjabi, English and Urdu, English and Vietnamese, all published by Ingham Yates)
Five Minutes Peace (Walker Books)
A Piece of Cake (Walker Books)
All in One Piece (Walker Books)
On the Way Home (Macmillan)
The Worst Witch (Puffin)
Whatever Next! (Macmillan)

Thematically linked picture books

Can't You Sleep, Little Bear? by Martin Waddell and Barbara Firth (Walker Books)
Goldilocks and the Three Bears